CREATURES WE CAN'T LIVE WITHOUT

We Need
BATS

HEATHER MOORE NIVER

PowerKiDS press

New York

Published in 2016 by The Rosen Publishing Group, Inc.
29 East 21st Street, New York, NY 10010

Copyright © 2016 by The Rosen Publishing Group, Inc.

All rights reserved. No part of this book may be reproduced in any form without permission in writing from the publisher, except by a reviewer.

First Edition

Editor: Caitie McAneney
Book Design: Mickey Harmon

Photo Credits: Cover (image), p. 16 Ivan Kuzmin/Shutterstock.com; cover, pp. 1, 3, 4, 8–10, 13, 16–17, 19–20, 22–24 (background) Click Bestsellers/Shutterstock.com; p. 5 Nicu Baicu/Shutterstock.com; pp. 6, 22 (bat) Eric Isselee/Shutterstock.com; pp. 7, 22 (bat) Kirsanov Valeriy Vladimirovich/Shutterstock.com; pp. 6–7 (background image) Umkehrer/Shutterstock.com; p. 8 (cannon) Jose Gil/Shutterstock.com; p. 9 (guano) Edward Kinsman/Science Source/Getty Images; p. 11 (Mexican free-tailed bat) Gilbert S Grant/Getty Images; p. 11 (big brown bat) Danita Delimont/Getty Images; p. 12 Visuals Unlimited, Inc./Joe McDonald/Getty Images; pp. 14–15 (background image) Kororiz Yuriy/Shutterstock.com; p. 15 (bat) Michael Lynch/Shutterstock.com; p. 17 (bat) Igor Chernomorchenko/Shutterstock.com; p. 17 (moth) jbmake/Shutterstock.com; p. 18 Bloomberg / Contributor/Gettty Images; p. 21 James H Robinson/Getty Images.

Library of Congress Cataloging-in-Publication Data

Niver, Heather Moore.
We need bats / by Heather Moore Niver.
p. cm. — (Creatures we can't live without)
Includes index.
ISBN 978-1-4994-0979-6 (pbk.)
ISBN 978-1-4994-1023-5 (6 pack)
ISBN 978-1-4994-1036-5 (library binding)
1. Bats — Juvenile literature. I. Niver, Heather Moore. II. Title.
QL737.C5 N58 2016
599.4—d23

Manufactured in the United States of America

CPSIA Compliance Information: Batch #WS15PK: For Further Information contact Rosen Publishing, New York, New York at 1-800-237-9932

CONTENTS

BATTY ABOUT BATS	4
NIGHT BITES	6
SPARKLY SCAT	8
AWESOME FOR AGRICULTURE	10
HELPING PLANTS GROW	13
SUPERSPIT	14
ECHOLOCATION	16
BATS IN DANGER	19
BUILDING FOR BATS	20
GLOSSARY	23
INDEX	24
WEBSITES	24

BATTY ABOUT BATS

Most of us duck out of the way when we see a bat swoop through the night air. Maybe we even scream in fear that it might bite us. But these furry flying beasts of the dark are interesting animals that we depend on.

Bats have a **reputation** for being nasty, germy bloodsuckers, but only vampire bats drink blood. Many bats fill their belly with fruit. They're called fruit-eating bats, and they help more fruit grow. Others are insectivores, which means they chow down on bugs. Without them, the world would be overrun by insects. We need these freaky, flying critters!

CREATURE CLUE

Bats are very clean animals. They spend a lot of time making sure their fur is soft. They almost never pass along diseases, or sicknesses, to other animals.

Bats eat all kinds of fruit, such as peaches, papayas, and watermelons.

NIGHT BITES

There are over 1,000 different species, or types, of bats. Bats are found everywhere on Earth except Antarctica. Many species live in tropical areas, which are hot and wet.

One bat can eat up to 1,000 mosquitoes in an hour! Bats also eat beetles, gnats, moths, and crickets.

Bats are the only flying **mammal** in the world. Flying squirrels can glide, but bats really fly! Their wings are made of thin, bendable skin stretched between their fingers, legs, and tail.

Bats are nocturnal, which means they're active at night. Many bats eat tiny insects, such as mosquitoes. Mosquitoes spread diseases such as malaria from person to person. Malaria causes fevers and sometimes even death. Without bats, mosquitoes would spread diseases to more people.

CREATURE CLUE

The thin skin in bat wings is a lot like the skin between frog toes. This skin, called webbing, helps frogs swim and bats fly! A bat's ability to fly helps it catch insects in the air.

SPARKLY SCAT

Some bats can eat their own body weight in insects in one night! Bats eat insects whole, including their exoskeleton, which is a hard, shiny outer covering. The exoskeleton is made out of matter called chitin, which is hard to **digest**. It comes out in the bat's scat, or droppings. That makes the scat of some species sparkle!

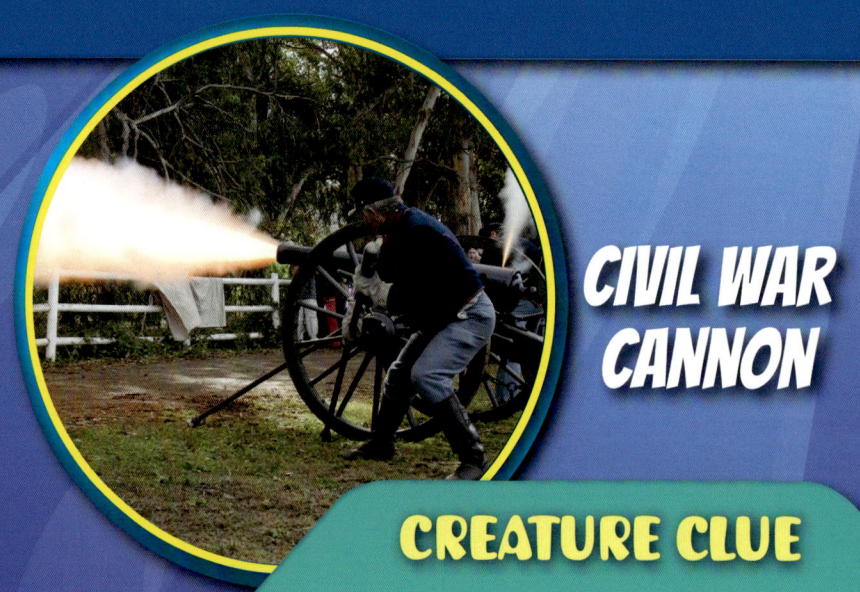

CIVIL WAR CANNON

CREATURE CLUE
Bat scat has been used for centuries. It was used to make gunpowder during the American Civil War.

People can use bat scat, or guano, to help their plants grow. Bat guano contains a chemical called nitrogen. This helps gardens and lawns grow bright and green. Plus, guano is natural and safer to use than other chemicals.

If each bat can eat its weight in insects, imagine how much guano is produced by a whole cave full of bats!

AWESOME FOR AGRICULTURE

In Texas, Mexican free-tailed bats protect crops by munching corn earworm moths, cotton bollworms, and tobacco budworms. Without bats, the moths would destroy crops, such as cotton, corn, and artichokes. Big brown bats make their meals from cucumber beetles, scarab beetles, stinkbugs, moths, and leafhoppers. Without hungry bats, these insects would destroy crops and spread disease.

With so many bats eating insects, Texas farmers can use fewer insecticides, or harmful chemicals, to kill the bugs. This saves time and money. More importantly, it's healthier for people and animals when farmers avoid using chemicals. Introducing bats to an area with pests is a natural way to save crops.

Some people call bats "vacuum cleaners" of the night sky! Just one colony of 150 big brown bats can eat enough cucumber beetles to keep them from laying 33 million rootworm eggs. Rootworms can seriously hurt corn crops.

BIG BROWN BAT

CREATURE CLUE

Researchers guess that Mexican free-tailed bats eat around 4 billion earworm moths every night. This may save cotton farmers in south-central Texas nearly $800,000 a year.

MEXICAN FREE-TAILED BAT

The Honduran white bat is an example of a fruit-eating bat. This tiny bat lives in rain forests and eats many plants. It lives in heliconia plants, whose leaves it uses as a tent.

HELPING PLANTS GROW

Bats have special jobs in their **ecosystems**. Fruit-eating bats play an important part in the growth of the fruit and flowers around them. Seeds from these meals leave their body in their scat. When the bats fly, they drop the seedy scat, which falls to the ground.

The seeds grow into new fruit trees! Some bats drink nectar, or the sweet, sticky liquid in flowers. As they drink from flowers, they get pollen on their faces. When they sip from the next blossom, that pollen rubs off on it. These bats help pollinate plants and help new fruit grow.

CREATURE CLUE

Bats pollinate many of the tropical plants humans eat, such as bananas, peaches, and avocados. Bats give us food!

SUPERSPIT

Vampire bats are usually thought of as scary bloodsuckers. Their large, supersharp teeth are perfect for biting through skin. Although they do drink blood, they usually bite animals, such as horses and cows. These South American bats rarely bite humans.

The vampire bat might be small, but scientists think it can be a huge help in medicine. A special chemical called draculin is found in vampire bat saliva, or spit. It helps keep blood from clotting, or getting too thick. Blood clots can lead to **strokes**, so scientists think the chemical might help treat stroke patients.

CREATURE CLUE

The chemical draculin was named after Dracula, a vampire in a story.

VAMPIRE BAT

Vampire bats use the draculin in their spit to make an animal's blood thinner so it's easier to drink.

15

ECHOLOCATION

Fruit and nectar eaters use their senses of smell and sight to hunt for their next meal. Insect-eating bats use a special process called **echolocation**. They send out high-pitched sounds that people can't hear. The sounds bounce off objects, and bats hear the echo. The echo tells them where something is, how big it is, and how fast it's moving.

CREATURE CLUE

Some bats have noses shaped like leaves. Leaf-nosed bats use their nose leaves to send out and receive echolocation sounds.

LEAF-NOSED BAT

Bats can fly fast and swoop through the air. Thanks to echolocation, they can sense where objects are.

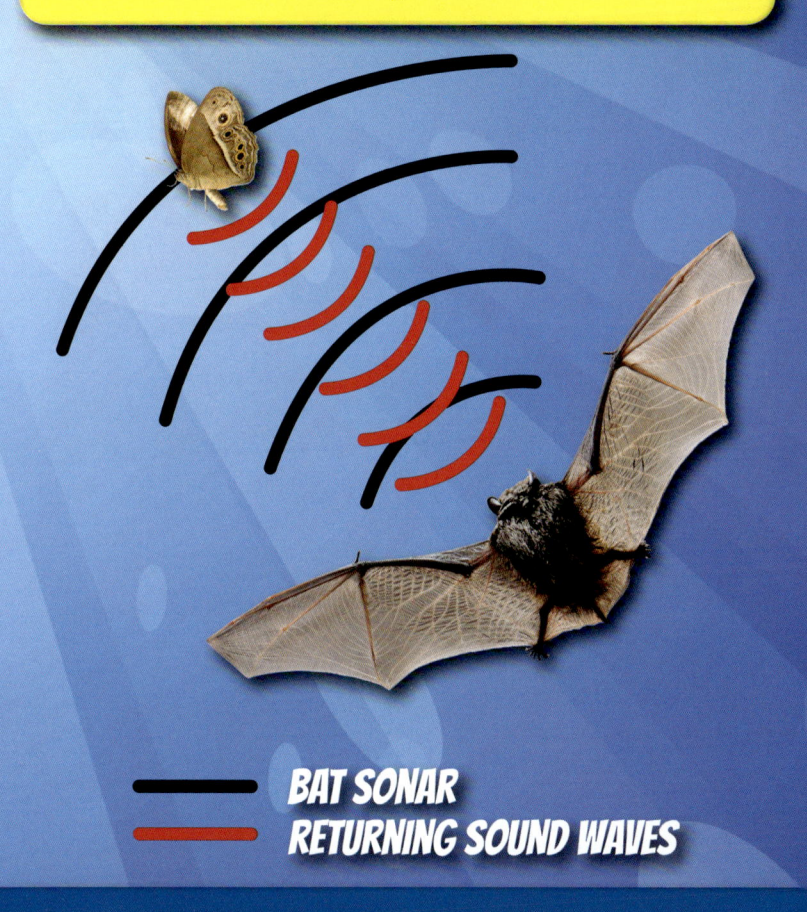

—— **BAT SONAR**
—— **RETURNING SOUND WAVES**

Some scientists are studying echolocation to create technology to help people who have poor eyesight or are blind. Special technology would send out signals to allow a person to sense what's around them, helping them move around more easily.

Scientists are working hard to figure out why North American bats are dying from a disease called white-nose syndrome. This disease appears as a white powder on bats' noses and other body parts when they're **hibernating**.

BATS IN DANGER

Bat species make up about 25 percent of all mammals. Unfortunately, some of these species are endangered, or at risk of dying out. This is bad news for their ecosystems and for us.

One reason some bats are becoming endangered is because their **habitats** are being ruined. Deforestation, or the cutting down of many trees, leaves many bats with no place to live. People are building wind turbines, or windmills, to create clean energy. But to **migrating** tree bats, turbines look like trees for resting. When bats fly into the turbine's spinning blades, they often die.

CREATURE CLUE

Scientists believe bats will suffer from climate change, or the change in weather patterns over time. Climate change could make bats leave their homes for better weather or may affect bat hibernation.

BUILDING FOR BATS

Entire ecosystems depend on bats, and we do, too. It's our responsibility to keep them from dying out. Scientists and engineers can find new ways to make wind turbines safer. People can speak out against destroying bat habitats.

How can you help save bats? Build them a bat house. Websites like the Bat Conservation Organization have simple plans for building bat houses. This can give bats a place to live and give you a chance to learn more about them.

Bats have been hanging around on Earth for more than 52 million years. Let's keep them around for a long time!

CREATURE CLUE

In the northeastern United States, you might see the big brown bat and the little brown bat. They're both common native species in the area.

You can build your own bat house or buy one. In most areas, bat houses should be at least 15 feet (4.6 m) above the ground. They should have 20 feet (6 m) of space around them.

Plants That Grow Because of Bats

- FIGS
- PASSION FRUIT
- ALMONDS
- PAPAYAS
- CASHEWS
- CACAO (CHOCOLATE)
- MANGOS
- GUAVAS
- AVOCADOS
- PEACHES

These are only a few of the plants that grow because of bats pollinating and dropping seeds!

GLOSSARY

digest: To break down food inside the body so the body can use it.

echolocation: A way of locating objects by making sounds that echo off the objects.

ecosystem: All the living things in an area.

habitat: The natural place where an animal or plant lives.

hibernate: To be in a sleep-like state for an extended period of time, usually during winter.

mammal: A warm-blooded animal that has a backbone and hair, breathes air, and feeds milk to its young.

migrate: To move from one area to another for feeding or having babies.

reputation: The views that are held about something or someone.

researcher: Someone who studies something closely.

stroke: A sudden blockage or break of a blood vessel in the brain.

INDEX

B
bat house, 20, 21
big brown bats, 10, 11, 20
blind, 17

C
climate change, 19

D
draculin, 14, 15

E
echolocation, 16, 17
ecosystems, 13, 19, 20

F
fruit, 4, 5, 13, 16
fruit-eating bats, 4, 12, 13

G
guano, 8, 9

H
habitats, 19, 20
hibernation, 18, 19
Honduran white bat, 12

I
insectivores, 4
insects, 4, 7, 8, 9, 10, 16

L
leaf-nosed bats, 16
little brown bat, 20

M
mammal, 7, 19
medicine, 14
Mexican free-tailed bats, 10, 11

N
nectar, 13, 16

P
pollinating, 13, 22

S
scat, 8, 9, 13
seeds, 13, 22
species, 6, 8, 19, 20

V
vampire bats, 4, 14, 15

W
white-nose syndrome, 18

WEBSITES

Due to the changing nature of Internet links, PowerKids Press has developed an online list of websites related to the subject of this book. This site is updated regularly. Please use this link to access the list: www.powerkidslinks.com/cwcl/bat